THE 2/26 BEFORE 9/11 @

THE WORLD TRADE CENTER

An Eyewitness Account

CLIFFORD N. OPURUM

Order this book online at www.trafford.com
or email orders@trafford.com

Most Trafford titles are also available at major online book retailers.

© Copyright 2024 Clifford N. Opurum.
All rights reserved. No part of this publication may be reproduced, stored in a
retrieval system, or transmitted, in any form or by any means, electronic, mechanical,
photocopying, recording, or otherwise, without the written prior permission of the author.

Print information available on the last page.

ISBN: 978-1-6987-1749-4 (sc)
ISBN: 978-1-6987-1750-0 (e)

Library of Congress Control Number: 2024918279

Because of the dynamic nature of the Internet, any web addresses or links contained in
this book may have changed since publication and may no longer be valid. The views
expressed in this work are solely those of the author and do not necessarily reflect the
views of the publisher, and the publisher hereby disclaims any responsibility for them.

Any people depicted in stock imagery provided by Getty Images are models, and such
images are being used for illustrative purposes only.
Certain stock imagery © Getty Images.

Trafford rev.   11/05/2024

www.trafford.com
North America & international
toll-free: 844-688-6899 (USA & Canada)
fax: 812 355 4082

Dedication

This eye-witness account is dedicated to all the victims of the two terrorist attacks at the World Trade Center in New York City on February 26, 1993 (2/26) and September 11, 2001 (9/11). It's also dedicated to all the souls lost at different locations in the United States from the 9/11 terrorist attacks. Particularly, it is dedicated to my five former colleagues at the New York Metropolitan Transportation Council (NYMTC) whose lives were abruptly taken away by terrorists on the 82nd Floor of Number One World Trade Center on September 11, 2001. More importantly, this book is dedicated to my Lord and Savior, my Redeemer, the King of kings and the Lord of lords, who graciously saved my life from the February 26, 1993 and the September 11, 2001 terrorists attacks at the World Trade Center through His divine protection and still small voice. To Him, and to Him alone be all the glory forever and ever. Amen!

Acknowledgement

First and foremost, I am very grateful to the Almighty God, who gave me the wisdom, strength, courage and the perseverance that enabled me to complete the manuscript for this book. My gratitude also goes to my dearly beloved "better half", my wife and sweetheart who ceaselessly put all the necessary pressure on me and challenged me to complete this book. She will often make a challenging remark to me (whenever I discuss the topic of this book with her) and say; Will you ever finish writing this book? I'm equally grateful to my dear children who have always encouraged me in my endeavors in their own special ways. I love them dearly.

Finally, I'm very thankful to my beloved parents who brought me into this world, and laid a very solid foundation for my future success before going home to be with the Lord. May their souls rest in perfect peace.

Preface

This book is based on a true, eyewitness account of what actually happened on that uneventful, gloomy, snowy and cold early afternoon on Friday February 26, 1993 at the New York City's, and America's famous landmark, the World Trade Center. Unquestionably, so much have been written on the terrorist attack on this fabulous architectural landmark, which occurred on September 11, 2001 but so little have been penned on the first terrorist attack (bombing) which occurred in approximately eight and a half years earlier on this magnificent landmark in America's most populous city and commercial capital also nicknamed the "Commercial Capital of the World".

As one of the living survivors of that first attack in 1993, I realized that the 9/11/2001 story would be incomplete without the knowledge and clear understanding of the tragic and sad events of 2/26/1993 which shook many Americans and citizens of other nations, who called the World Trade Center their home for business. Indeed, should the various local, regional and national security agents and authorities in the United State have taken the

February 26, 1993 attack very seriously in the same way and extent that they did for the September 11, 2001, the second attack would have been avoided. I also thought that it would be morally and psychologically unfair to the thousands of men, women and children who were directly or indirectly victimized by that particular incident which took six innocent lives and left, hundreds of people wounded, many traumatized, and several families devastated, in its aftermath. You will agree with me that one life lost, is one too many. Some people would only agree with this statement only "when the pain strikes home".

Downtown Manhattan (a heavily commercialized section of New York City), and particularly, the peripheries of the World Trade Center, including the World Financial Center and the Wall Street and adjoining streets, were seriously shaken and in fact in pandemonium following that attack. It was indeed a horrific and unimaginable event that took everyone at the Trade Center on that very day by surprise. Number One World Trade Center (1 WTC or the North Tower) and Number Two World Trade Center (2 WTC or the South Tower), popularly known as the Twin Towers, represented a major bearing point from most locations in the New York-New Jersey-Connecticut Tri-State Region in the northeast of the nation. Standing at one hundred and ten stories tall, with the North Tower equipped with Antenna spire and the South Tower with a helicopter landing pad, the Twin Towers dwarfed the rest of the buildings in and around the region.

The February 26, 1993 bombing of the World Trade Center happened unexpectedly between 12 noon and 2 p.m. as most of the workers and residents of the complex were returning from their lunch break. Within minutes of a very loud and explosive sound, thick smoke rose quickly from the basement of the North Tower and filled the hallways and stairways while the elevators automatically shut down within the entire complex. What followed inside the Towers thereafter is something you would not want to see nor experience. It was indeed scary, tragic, and horrific. You really wouldn't want to be a part of it. Certain events are better heard as fictions rather than realities.

This book is written for everyone who abhors terrorism and all manner of evil against humanity. It is written so that all my co-survivors from that horrible incident, and families of those six individuals whose lives were abruptly cut short and taken away on that dark Friday will know that they have not been forgotten and that a life lost is one too many. I'm hoping that you enjoy reading this book and reflect or imagine the nature of the physical and social environments of New York City and the entire nation as it was on February 26, 1993 and September 11, 2001. We must unite and be in one accord as we fight the evil of terrorism, because terrorism anywhere is terrorism everywhere. The evil of terrorism all across the globe must be brought to an end and the ungodly evildoers must one day answer to the one who created us all, the Almighty God. Any terrorist attack in any nation is an attack on all humanity. It is imperative therefore, that we join forces with a common agenda and deal with the forces of evil which undoubtably exist in our society. All in all, we understand that one soul lost is one too many and that there is no peace for the wicked.

Professor Clifford N. Opurum, PhD, MCIT

About The Author

$\mathfrak{C}$lifford N. Opurum, Ph.D., MCIT is a seasoned Professor of Transportation Planning & Engineering, Economics, and Management. He currently teaches for the City University of New York (CUNY), and Pratt Institute (Pratt University) in New York City, where he has been teaching since 2006 and 2008, respectively. He has also taught at two campuses of the State University of New York (SUNY New Paltz and F.I.T. SUNY). In the 2008/9 Academic Year, Dr. Opurum taught various micro and macroeconomics courses (including Economics of Globalization) as a full-time Visiting Assistant Professor of Economics at SUNY-New Paltz, and in 2009, at F.I.T.-SUNY as an Adjunct Faculty (Economics). He was also an Adjunct Instructor of Business Administration and Management at Briarcliffe College in Bethpage, New York, Adjunct Professor of Management at Berkeley College in New York City, and a visiting faculty at the College of New Rochelle, New York.

Dr. Opurum is the author of the award-winning Automated Fare Collection System & Urban Public

Transportation: An Economic and Management Approach to Urban Transit Systems. He is also the author of the spiritually inspiring Forty Days of Fasting & Prayers in the Biblical Context: A Kingdom Message for Believers and Unbelievers, and the international business-oriented Globalization and Regional Integration: The ECOWAS Model, among his other published works. His unpublished peer-reviewed research papers include "A Review of the Relationship Between Public Transportation Pricing and Travel Demand: An Exploratory Study", which was presented at the 2006 International Business Conference in Orlando, Florida held by the Society for the Advancement of Management. Some of his work-in-progress research papers include "Transportation Alternative Energy and Social Entrepreneurship", and "Entrepreneurship and Small Business Development".

In 2008, Dr. Opurum presented a research paper titled "Regional Economic Integration" at the First World Diaspora Conference sponsored by the First World Chapter of the State University of New York at New Paltz Alumni Association and the Departments of Black Studies and Foreign Languages, and the Latin-American Studies. He was also a Special Guest Speaker at the State University of New York at New Paltz Students in Free Enterprise (SIFE) event held on November 7, 2008, where he delivered a special keynote speech on "Entrepreneurship and Small Business Development".

In addition to his other academic and professional credentials, Dr. Opurum holds a Diploma (B.A. Hon.) in Transport Studies from University of London, England (1982), a Master of Science (Marine Transportation Management) from State University of New York Maritime College (1985), M.A. (Economics) from Fordham University, New York (1987), Master of Science (Transportation Planning & Engineering) from the Polytechnic University, New York (1994), and a Ph.D. (Transport Studies) from the University of Leeds, England (2005). His professional memberships include Corporate Member of The Chartered Institute of Transport (MCIT), Associate Member of the Institute of Transportation Administration, former Member of the Institute of Transportation Engineers, and Member, Society for the Advancement of Management (SAM). Dr. Opurum's research interest is in the areas of international/global business, strategic management, economics, sea, land and air transportation management, planning and engineering, and urban policy. He has attended several international business management and other academic conferences (including one organized by the Federal Reserve Bank New York at its corporate offices in New York City), and presented and reviewed some research papers at some of the conferences he attended.

Prior to his teaching appointments, Dr. Opurum held several management positions in both the public and private sectors within the New York Metropolitan Region most of which are in the transportation industry. From 1991 to 1993, he authored the New York Metropolitan Area Regional Transportation Status Report as the Project Manager for the New York-New Jersey-Connecticut Tri-State Regional Transportation and Demographics Monitoring Project at the New York Metropolitan Transportation Council (NYMTC) of the New York State Department of Transportation (NYS DOT). He was a member of the New York City Transportation Task Force and Senior Citizens Transportation Advisory Committee (1988-91), which designed and implemented the New York City premier Para-transit Program otherwise known as the Access-A-Ride, during the administrations of Mayors Edward I. Koch and David N. Dinkins. During that same period, he worked for the New York City Department for The Aging (DFTA) as a Community Coordinator (Transportation and Social Services) and subsequently, as a Program Officer (Contract Manager).

In 1994, Dr. Opurum worked with the consulting firm of Louis Berger & Associates, Incorporated as a Senior Transportation Planner at the company's East Orange,

New Jersey corporate offices, where he supervised field assignments on public transportation and highway improvement projects under contracts with government agencies ((including the Federal Highway Administration (FHA) and New York City Transit Authority (NYCTA)). He was also a Transportation Planner (Project Manager, Ridership Analysis and Reports) from 1997 to 2004 with the Metro-North Railroad of the New York Metropolitan Transportation Authority (MTA).

Dr. Opurum's extra-curriculum activities include doing God's work as an Ordained Deacon, a licensed Chaplain, and a Chorister. By the grace of God, he narrowly survived the first terrorist attack at the World Trade Center in New York City on February 26, 1993 where he worked for NYMTC of the NYS DOT (then located on the 82nd Floor of Number One World Trade Center). He would have been a victim of the September 11, 2001 terrorist attack had he not listened to the still small voice of God in 1994, and this, indeed, motivated him to write this book. He is married and lives in New York with his family.

Contents

Dedication...v

Acknowledgement.. vii

Preface...ix

About The Author xiii

Chapter 1   Introduction 1

Chapter 2   The Absolute Dark Moment on
            February 26, 1993................................ 18

Chapter 3   The 2/26 Post-Bombing Period: The
            Years Between 2/26 And 9/11 26

Chapter 4   The September 11, 2001 Attacks 29

Chapter 5   The Socioeconomic Implications
            of The 2/26 And 9/11 Terrorists
            Bombings And Attacks 40

Chapter 6   Summing It Up....................................46

References/Further Information..........................55

Chapter One

Introduction

What many people, both in and outside the United States of America, do not know regarding the World Trade Center terror attacks is that before September 11, 2001 (otherwise known world-wide as the **9/11**) there was February 26, 1993 (otherwise referred to as the **2/26** in this eyewitness account). In other words, before **9/11** was 2/26. These different dates featured two different uneventful incidences but with similar pains and agonies including, but not limited to loss of innocent lives, personal injuries, property damages and economic set-backs. However, the commemorative events of 9/11 have over-shadowed those of 2/26 till this day.

Most of the younger generations born few years before the event and those born in the immediate period following the event have little, if any, knowledge of this awful and outrageous incident that drastically impacted many families in and around the Tri-State Region of New

1

York-New Jersey- Connecticut in the Northeastern Region of the United States of America and beyond.

The Year 2024 marked the 31st Anniversary of the first terrorist bombing of the World Trade Center. In just over 31 years ago, some Islamic extremists bombed the World Trade Center thereby, destroying millions, if not billions of dollars worth of properties (and infrastructures), cutting short six innocent lives, and injuring more than one thousand people. The first terrorist attack on the World Trade Center, located in the Central Business District (CBD) of the Borough of Manhattan in New York City (a.k.a. New York, New York), USA on February 26, 1993 is a story that has not been fully narrated. That evil terrorist act occurred when a truck which was fully-loaded with explosives was remotely detonated below the North Tower (Tower One or One World Trade Center) in the World Trade Center Complex at exactly 12:17 p.m. Eastern Standard Time (EST) on February 26, 1993 by demonic agents and cowards otherwise called Islamic extremists or terrorists.

Terrorism, as defined by the Collins English Dictionary[1], is a systematic use of violence and intimidation to achieve some goal. These goals are usually selfish and with some inhumane ulterior motives in nature. It is the act of terrorizing another individual(s), group(s), neighborhood(s), etc. A terrorist is therefore a person who employs terror or terrorism for his/her selfish ulterior motives. To terrorize is to coerce or control by violence, fear, threats, etc. Given these definitions, it's very obvious that any act of terrorism is without doubt very inhumane and therefore cannot, should not. and will never be condoned at any time, at any place. It is very demonic and evil by itself, and a terrorist is a satanic agent, a lover of evil, and an enemy of peace, to say the least. Simply put, there is no justification for terrorism and anyone caught in such act, must be brought to justice.

The motive of the attack, as the United States Federal security/law- enforcement agents later identified, was a back-lash against American foreign policy, and U.S. support of Israel in the latter's issues with its neighboring Palestine. Besides the six innocent lives that were lost on that day, 1,042 persons were seriously injured (including me). I miraculously survived the February 26, 1993 bombing; I was there on the 82nd Floor of One World Trade Center when it suddenly and unexpectedly happened. I suffered from suffocation, and breathing problem due to serious smoke inhalation as the result of that terrorist bombing. Subsequently, and following thorough investigations by the U.S. Federal security agents in the aftermath of the bombing, the perpetrators of the bombing were identified. The vagabonds involved in the incident include the following agents of evil and their co-conspirators: Ramzi

Yousef, Eyad Ismoil, Ahmed Ajaj, Mohammad Salameh, Abdul Yasin, Mahmoud Abou Halima, and Nidal Ayyad. The story you are about to read is a true, unadulterated eyewitness account of what happened on that uneventful, snowy Friday afternoon in the month of February 1993, in the heart of the winter of 1992/1993.

We often take things for granted and particularly, when we are not directly affected by an action or incident of a tragic or catastrophic nature. Of the six lives that were lost on that day, four were personnel of the Port Authority of New York and New Jersey (PANY&NY), the Landlord (owner) of the World Trade Center, which itself was the world's famous landmark with elegant architectural structures. The name of these six individuals whose lives were abruptly cut short on that sorrowful, snowy day are inscribed in panel N-73 of the North Pool at the 9/11 Memorial, the exact location where the North Tower formerly stood. The deceased six include five males and one female (the youngest) and their names and their respective ages as inscribed on Panel N-73 of the North Pool are as follows: John DiGiovanni (45), Robert "Bob" Kirkpatrick (61), Stephen Knapp (47), Bill Macko (57), Wilfredo Mercado (37) and Monica Rodriguez Smith (35).

It is indeed true that when we are not the one involved in an incident, everything about it would sound to us as a fiction or a fairy tale. There is a popular saying in a particular region in the African Continent which states that when someone else's coffin is carried to the burial place, strangers see it as a mere log of dried, useless palm tree trunk. In other words, the news of death, for instance, does not move most people unless they are members of the bereaved family or that they have some form of relationship or the other with the deceased individual.

Many individuals who are familiar with the story of the September 11, 2001 terrorist attack (a.k.a. 9/11) at the World Trade Center (New York City), the Pentagon (Washington D.C.), and in Pennsylvania, have no idea of the first attack on the World Trade Center in approximately eight and half years earlier. (For those who do not know what the Pentagon represents, it is the military headquarters or the Defense Headquarters of the United States of America, representing the world's most powerful military force). It is doubtless to say that millions of people who were born after February 26, 1993 have not heard about the 2/26 terrorist bombing at the World Trade Center. Indeed, several people who were born before that historic date do not know of this first terrorist attack.

Recently, on February 26 2018, the Twenty-Fifth (25th) Anniversary of the first terrorist attack on American soil was marked but not celebrated as some would describe that occasion. Any use of the word "celebration" to remember such an evil act amounts to nothing but lack of wisdom.

The picture of the horrific incident at the World Trade Center on February 26, 1993 is one that will ever remain fresh in my memory as long as I live. But I will never cease to give thanks to God for saving my life on that horrific day, and I will remain faithful and grateful to Him.

Though I have forgiven the barbarians who committed that horrific, evil act, forgetting that incident have been a struggle for the past thirty-one years. It was indeed a nightmare. As Julius Caesar once stated, "the evils that men do lives after them", and believe it or not, it is a fact that there is no peace for the wicked. This means that no one who is in one way or the other connected with the evil plans and actions that took thousands of innocent souls on 2/26/93 and 9/11/01 will not have peace, except, of cause, if they confess their sins and completely repent of their evil acts. Because they have chosen evil over good, evil shall not depart from them for the rest of their lives except they show true repentance. The guilt of knowing the fact about the millions of innocent lives they have destroyed will be enough to keep them miserable and restless for the rest of their lives. Assuming any of them is still remaining alive, sleepless nights will cloud the rest of their days.

Oftentimes in my quiet moments, I would pause and begin to reminiscent and recall my memories of that outrageous, ungodly and demonic event. In fact, I would sometimes begin to wonder where I would have been, or what I physically would have looked like, if I had ignored the voice of God as He warned me to resign from my comfortable, secured New York State Government civil service (public service) employment as the Project Manager of the New York-New Jersey-Connecticut Tri-State Region Transportation & Demographics Monitoring Project, and leave that environment as soon as I could. I also heard the same voice whispering to me that I should not worry about securing another job when I leave since He would provide a better job for me, but I could lose my life if I stay.

Without doubting God, I acted like Prophet Abraham in the Bible (Genesis, Chapter 12), who left his comfortable home, his kindreds and possessions for an unknown territory at age 75 as God told him to do. However, my obedience to the voice of God was misinterpreted by my colleagues and supervisors (at that time and even till this day) as an act of disloyalty and disobedience to the administration. But I prayed for them that God may open their spiritual eyes so they could see in the same way that I did and have continued to do.

One thing each and every one of us must understand is the fact that acquiring money and accumulating wealth is not all there is to life. It is neither a guarantee for happiness nor healthy living and we definitely cannot buy peace with money. We really have to be alive, and remain physically and spiritually strong in order for us to enjoy the wealth we accumulate here on earth. We all need a discerning mind from God so we may act upon His Word when He speaks to us. To have a discerning mind is a gift from God, and it is divine wisdom, which is knowledge rightly applied. It belongs to everyone who hears the still small voice of God when He speaks to us, and then obey Him without hesitation.

The 2/26 terrorist attack at the World Trade Center in New York City took the lives of six innocent souls within the entire complex. But the 9/11 terrorist attack on that same complex killed six of my former colleagues who worked with me in the same office space on the 82nd Floor East in Number One World Trade Center. These individuals were among the 2,797 innocent souls that were lost in that horrific and satanic incident on that day that shook all of us, and sent chills down our spines. It's indeed even more heart-breaking to know that of almost two thousand, eight hundred lives that were lost on that uneventful day, 343 were fire fighters, who sacrificed their own lives in attempts and efforts to save the lives of their fellow human-beings. In addition, several security personnel, from and outside of New York also lost their lives due to the attack. It was indeed tragic.

Unquestionably, so much have been written on the terrorist attack on this fabulous and state-of-the-art architectural landmark which took place on September 11,

2001 but so little have been penned on the first terrorist attack (bombing) which occurred in approximately eight and a half years earlier on this same magnificent landmark in America's Commercial Capital nicknamed the "Commercial Capital of the World".

Prior to the February 26, 1993 bombing, the ambience of the environment in and around this world's famous architectural complex were so inviting, to say the least. A walk from the World Trade Center across the magnificent and architecturally designed pedestrian walkway to the World Financial Center (WFC) located on the bank of the great Hudson River was indeed very relaxing, recreating and rejuvenating. Together, the World Trade Center and the World Financial Center represented an extra-ordinary tourist attraction within the "Commercial Capital of the World" (New York, New York).

The World Trade Center, a bi-state facility, is owned by the Port Authority of New York & New Jersey (PANY&NJ). For those who didn't have the opportunity to see the original (old) World Trade Center before it was utterly destroyed by the enemies of progress, you may want to know that the World Trade Center was an attractive architectural landmark made up of seven magnificent buildings located in the lower west end of the Borough of Manhattan, a.k.a., New York, New York (meaning New York County of New York State).

In other words, within the complex referred to as the World Trade Center, there were Number One, Number Two, Number Three, Number Four, Number Five, Number Six and Number Seven World Trade Center addresses before the 9/11 terrorist attacks. Prominent among these buildings were Number One WTC (the North Tower) and Number Two WTC (the South Tower), which towered over the rest of the buildings in and around the complex at the heights of 1,368 feet (417 meters) and 1,362 feet (415 meters), respectively. (See figures 1 and 2, and the front cover. Courtesy of Wikipedia, the free Encyclopedia.) These two extra-ordinary architectural structures were popularly known to New Yorkers as the "Twin Towers". Each of them stood and towered at 110 stories with observatory decks accessible to the public and a helicopter landing pad (helipad) at the top of Number Two World Trade Center.

The Twin Towers were the major targets of the terrorists in each of the two different attacks of February 26, 1993 (a.k.a. 2/26) and September 11, 2001 (a.k.a. 9/11). The alternative names for Number One World Trade Center are 1 WTC, North Tower, WTC 1, Building A, Building 1, and Tower 1. For Number Two World Trade Center, the names include 2 WTC, South Tower, WTC 2, Building B, Building 2 and Tower 2.

1 World Trade Center

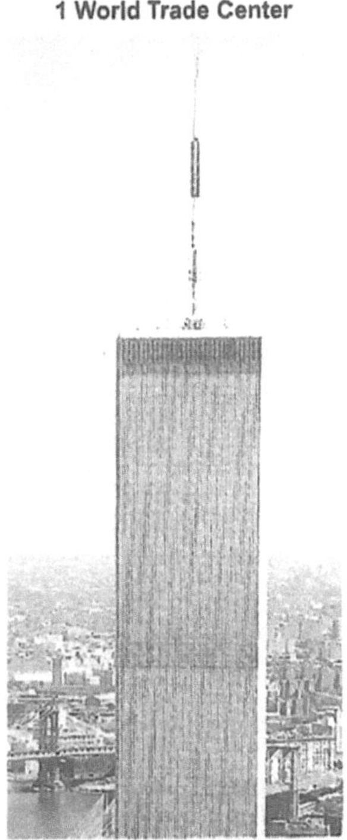

Figure 1: The Original World Trade Center's North Tower (1 WTC) pictured in the Summer of 2001. (Courtesy of Wikipedia, The Free Encyclopedia)

Based on the information obtained from Wikipedia, at their completion in 1973 (with the North Tower completed earlier in 1972), the Twin Towers represented the world's tallest buildings at that time. Built with several millions of dollars, approximately $400 million or about $3.80 billion in 2023 dollars, the Twin Towers stood for roughly twenty-eight years before their destruction; it was indeed a painful loss.

2 World Trade Center

Figure 2: The Original World Trade Center's South Tower (2 WTC) pictured in the Summer of 2001. (Courtesy of Wikipedia, The Free Encyclopedia)

Prior to the completion of the Twin Towers, another skyscraper and a major architectural landmark, the Empire State Building (located in the mid-section of Manhattan in New York City), represented the tallest building on the East Coast of the United States at the height of 1,250 feet. Built during the Great Depression at a total cost of $40 million, the Empire State Building was opened in 1931 with 73 elevators (lifts), 1,860 steps, and top most habitable floor located high up on the 86th Floor. The tallest building in the United States is the Willis Tower (formerly known as the Sears Tower) in Chicago, Illinois. At a height of 1,451 feet, it surpassed the original Twin Towers of the

World Trade Center. However, the current world's tallest skyscraper is the Burj Khalifa (meaning the Tower of Khalifa) in Dubai, United Arad Emirates (UAE), with a height of 2,717 feet and was completed in 2010 at a total cost of $1.5 billion (New York Post, Tuesday January 5, 2010, and Wikipedia, the free Encyclopedia).

The original World Trade Center also included several other facilities: an underground shopping mall and garages, banks, a world-class, international standard hotel, restaurants and balconies, and underground train stations (including, one that connected Downtown Manhattan with parts of Northern New Jersey, the PATH Train). Each of the Twin Towers housed several multinational, international and local businesses as well as government offices including offices of the New York Metropolitan Transportation Council (NYMTC) and the Port Authority of New York and New Jersey (PANY&NJ), the Landlord of the World Trade Center.

On each floor of the Twin Towers were mini-streets with signs which provided adequate directions to visitors and without which one could easily get lost inside the building. (Once in a while, visitors to the Twin Towers will go round and round in circles looking for their destination inside the buildings.) Hence, a visitor can easily become disoriented or feel lost on any given floor in either of the Twin Towers.

I could reminiscent how life used to be at the World Trade Center in those peaceful, non-terror, good old days. At lunch time on each weekday, the Grand Plaza of the WTC complex could be likened to the Assembly Hall of the United Nations Headquarters (located on the east side of Midtown Manhattan on the bank of the East River). People of all colors, tribes, tongues, of various racial and ethnic backgrounds, of different sizes and shapes, and of different nationalities and religious creeds will converge at the plaza to socialize and recreate as they listened and enjoyed free music entertainments from freelance musicians while they ate their takeaway lunches (which New Yorkers are accustomed to). Here, you see and understand the reason why New York City (the commercial capital) is referred to as the "Melting Pot". It was really amazing to see New Yorkers relaxing and enjoying a peaceful atmosphere in one of the world's busiest cities, and free from terrorism and terrors. May we never take peace and freedom for granted; money cannot buy them.

Those who know New Yorkers very well will agree that we are always in a rush; always running instead walking and no matter the distance, never pausing to admire and enjoy the magnificence of several architectural landmarks that add to the beauty and ambience of the great City of New York. Particularly, the Borough of Manhattan (where the World Trade Center is situated), with its official address as New York, New York, which actually represents New York County in New York State, is also nicknamed the "Commercial Capital of the World".

Spending a few minutes of your time to observe people as they do their things in the streets of New York can be so much fun. During a particular lunch break in the summer of 1992, I observed an elderly couple standing in the line in a fast food, pizza restaurant near the Trade Center as they waited for their turn (on a line as long as the Mississippi River, figuratively speaking) to purchase their own slices of pizza. When it reached their turn to grab their own slices, the pizza man took two slices of peperoni pizza from the pie and was horridly presenting them to the elderly couple but they rejected it and asked if the slices could be cooked a little longer and be well done. The pizza man did not waste any second to ignore them and offered the same slices of pizza to the next customer in the line by shouting the word "Next!" To the greatest surprise of these elderly couple, that other customer quickly and happily grabbed the two slices as they were. Welcome to New York, New York (the core of the "Big Apple").

Following my observations, I immediately concluded without further evidence that those elderly couple were not from New York (they are not New Yorkers); judging from their accent, I guessed they came from one of the quiet, more relaxed states in the southern part of the country where people are not so much in a hurry to get the pizza out of the oven. There's really so much fun to be a New Yorker, and many New Yorkers find it very difficult and uninteresting to live elsewhere in quieter environments.

This book is written for everyone who abhors terrorism and all manner of evil against humanity. It is written so that all my co-survivors from that horrible incident, and families of those six individuals whose lives were abruptly cut short and taken away on that dark Friday will know that they have not been forgotten and that a life lost is one too many. In addition to the fatalities, there were hundreds of casualties who were rushed to nearby health facilities, including the Beeckman Downtown Hospital where many of victims including myself were revived from serious smoke inhalation and suffocation. I could recall waking up on a stretcher at the hospital with oxygen mask over my face, and indeed, I was disoriented for several minutes.

A combined team of federal and local law enforcement agents arrested six suspects who are connected with the attack. The aim of this book is also to present the true, eyewitness account of the events of the February 26, 1993 terrorist bombing of the World Trade Center to many who do not know of that scary and demonic incident, and to recommend appropriate security measures necessary to prevent further terrorist attacks to the magnitude of the 2/26/93 and 9/11/01 attacks. Particularly, it is written so that the younger generations who were too young to witness the incidence or were born afterwards would have another piece of New York and the United States history added to their existing knowledge.

While structuring this book, I thought of narrating a true eyewitness story that would be very simple and easy to read and comprehend by anyone interested in knowing the facts about the act of terrorism at the world's famous landmark in less than a decade before the 9/11 attacks. Chapter One, Introduction, presents a general background (an overview) of the terrorist attacks on February 26, 1993 and September 11, 2001. In Chapter Two, the events which preceded a period of complete darkness in Number One World Trade Center (WTC) are presented. It also includes the dramatic activities observed at the New York Beeckman Downtown Hospital, where most of the casualties of the February 26, 1993 were treated and cared for. Chapter Three features the social and economic environments in the years between the February 26, 1993 and September 11, 2001 terrorist attacks.

Chapter Four features the events of the September 11, 2001 terrorist attacks and their aftermaths. Chapter Five deals with the socioeconomic implications of the 2/26 and 9/11 bombings in New York City in particular and in the United States in general. In the final chapter, Chapter 6, we sum up the unbelievable tale of terrorist attacks and eyewitness account.

Chapter Two

The Absolute Dark Moment on February 26, 1993

Like every other Friday in typical winter months in New York City, a.k.a. the "Big Apple", Friday February 26, 1993 started as a normal winter day. It was a day that the Lord made and blessed and most people started the day with joy and gladness as they enjoyed the beauty of it. This was until the sudden and unthinkable event happened later that day. The usual pattern of the early morning commute was the order of the day with the traditional or customary traffic congestion and the associated noise pollutions which symbolize life in urban centers. Traditionally, February has been the coldest month of the year in New York, and February 1993 was not an exception to the norm.

Although it began to snow later on in the day, but the presence of snow coupled with a very low winter-like temperature helped tremendously to reduce the devastating impact of the terrorist attack on the Trade Center on that day. It could have been worse otherwise. All together the snow and the low temperature on that very day were, indeed, a blessing in disguise. Otherwise, many more lives could have been lost, and several more casualties could have been recorded from the multiple effects of the heat, smoke and fire that followed immediately after the bomb explosion that occurred later on that day.

At approximately 12:17 p.m. on Friday, February 26, 1993 most of the workers at One World Trade Center, including myself were returning to work from lunch break with some of us still trying to get into our offices when the tide suddenly turned. On the 82nd Floor of Number One WTC (the North Tower) where my office was located, the first unusual thing we sensed was the smell of a fire. What followed in the next few seconds was very thick smoke which started quickly and gradually filled up and clouded the hallways, and then the office spaces. At that moment, we were instructed to soak either a handkerchief or sheets of paper towel and use them to cover our noses and mouths to minimize or prevent serious smoke inhalation that was unquestionably eminent.

Meanwhile, all the elevators in the building had stopped operating as the power supply was already shut-off automatically for safety reasons. Immediately following this, there was so much pandemonium in the hallways of the 82nd Floor of Number 1 World Trade Center where I was located at that very moment. Unable to take any of our personal belongings from the offices with us, everyone raced for their lives towards the nearest exit. (Don't forget that we were on the 82nd Floor at that very moment.) It was a case of swim or sink as no one in our survival race group knew what was happening and all you could see on people's faces was fear and anxiety. It was a walk of faith in the midst of a pandemonium and confusion. The thought that kept coming to my mind at that very moment was the promise God made to those that put their trust in Him that they will never be confounded, and that when we dwell in His secret places, we shall abide under His shadow (The Shadow of the Almighty God, our protector).

As you read this chapter, it is imperative for you to understand the absolute truth that God can use anything or anyone to do what He wants to do, including saving lives. When miracles take place or are manifested in our lives, we must not cease nor forget to give honor to whom honor is due, and that is none other but the Almighty God, the Miracle-working God. Most individuals who don't believe in God, a.k.a. the unbelievers will simply say that they are lucky when a miracle takes place in and around them. We must indeed change the way we think and be realistic and to know that a divine power is behind every fortune we experience in our lives. Let's be realistic and believe in the power of divine authority. This chapter could also be captioned: "The Cellular Phone, The Pregnant Woman, and The Dark Stairway".

At approximately 12:18 p.m. on February 26, 1993, as most of the thousands of people who work and do their businesses in Number One World Trade Center were returning from their well-deserved lunch breaks to their various offices in this 110-story tower, a very loud, and terrifying noise of several decibels, which shook parts of the complex, was heard both within and several miles away from the location. That explosion sent thick smoke filled with soot and other particulate matters (PM), from the basement to the top floor of the building and beyond. The presence of very thick soot and these microscopic, particulate matters in the smoke due to the sudden and incomplete combustion of the different types of fuel substances did more harm to the health of the victims. Hence, the outbreak of cancer-related illnesses to many who were in and around the vicinity of the WTC even after several weeks and months of the incident

Subsequently, there was a great pandemonium in the entire complex as people started to choke and suffocate from the dual effects of soot and smoke, and as they desperately sort exit from the complex through smoke-filled stairways. On that fateful Friday afternoon in the winter of 1993, the Omnipresent God miraculously saved thousands of lives (including mine). Thousands of people were trapped in smoke-filled stairways, with temperatures of not less than 150 degrees Fahrenheit (150° F). With respect to extreme temperatures and human beings, we must understand that thirty-two degrees Fahrenheit (32° F) represents the melting point of ice and that cold water boils at a temperature of two hundred- and twelve-degrees Fahrenheit (212° F) and of course, physicists and chemists will understand exactly what this means in terms of human health.

Given the above scenario, one can Imagine how it felt to be trapped in such a stairway that was also absolutely dark and filled with soot. The stairway was so dark to the point that no one could see the person standing next to them. All you could hear in that stairway (which is just one of the several stairways in the building) were voices of people crying and screaming as much as they could for help. It was indeed very suffocating, extremely hot, and terrifying to the extent that you wouldn't even wish your enemy to be there, to say the least. The fact that we came out of that horrific environment was nothing other than divine intervention. It was indeed nothing but God factor. Also, the fact that the pregnant woman (who, I believe was the only one among us with a cellular phone) was able to dial the emergency 911 phone number for help proves that there is a miracle-working, promise-keeping, Omnipresent God who watches over us.

I believe that the pregnant Caucasian woman I'm referring to in this eyewitness account, and who God used to save many lives (including myself) on February 26, 1993 also survived that horrific act of the terrorists. I also believe that the baby she was carrying also survived and if so, would have already celebrated his/her Thirty-first (31th) Birthday as of March 2024; following the Thirty-first (31th) Anniversary of 2/26/93 terrorist bombing of the World Trade Center. That's a miracle baby indeed and I would wish that he/she was named "Miracle" or "Angel" since it was because of him/her that the mother was carrying a cellular phone because she was nearing her delivery date. We must understand that in the 1990s, cellular phones were not so common for the working-class group in our society. It was seen as a luxury and only a few privileged individuals were able to afford one; I personally had none.

It's very imperative to understand that the safety system at the World Trade Center is designed to shut-off the elevators in the event of a major explosion. Also, what those barbarians and cowards who carried out that evil act did not know is that the foundations of the Twin Towers (Number One and Number Two World Trade Center) are linked with several cables to the bedrock of the lower Hudson River, which borders the states of New York and

New Jersey. Therefore, anything that can pull down any of those two towers will be capable of sinking a large part of the southern tip of New York County (Manhattan, a.k.a New York, New York or New York County in New York State).

The architectural design of each of the Twin Towers included several stairways designed to ensure adequate level of safe evacuation of their occupants in case of any emergency. This is in addition to several elevators located in each of the buildings, with most of them providing several express services between the first floor and the seventy-second (72nd) floor. I rode in those elevators on a daily basis on weekdays until the time of the attack. The Grand Plaza of the World Trade Centre prior to the February 26, 1993 terrorist attack could have been appropriately nicknamed the "All Nations Grand Plaza" or "All Tribes and Tongues Grand Plaza". Usually, on normal summer seasons before that barbaric act, the plaza featured various entertainers (mostly musicians) and cheerful, grateful audiences made up of people from various cultural and ethnic backgrounds, and of different nationalities and indeed the entire scenery with its ambience, reflected What New York City represented; the "Melting Pot". It was such a beautiful and inviting plaza until the agents of evil destroyed it. It is very obvious that anyone who hates beauty with its ambience and any good thing for that matter, such things will never come to them

Like every other Friday during the summer months when most employers in New York City allow their employees to come to work in casual attire in those days, otherwise known to many New Yorkers as "dress down Friday", majority of the employees who worked at the World Trade Center were all in their casuals on February 26, 1993.

Chapter Three

The 2/26 Post-Bombing Period: The Years Between 2/26 And 9/11

The mastermind (or architect) of the February 26, 1993 terrorist bombing at the World Trade Center, Ramzi Yousef (who was only 24 years old at that time), was later arrested by the United States federal authorities and sentenced to a life prison term plus 240 years. This barbarian and heartless murderer called Yousef, was later sent to serve a life sentence at a federal super-maximum-security prison in Colorado, USA. It's very much believed that Ramzi Yousef carried out this atrocity alone by himself. Nevertheless, he was not a "lone soldier"; he had several other "co-conspirators".

The months and years following the 2/26 bombing, were nothing but a period of fear, anxiety, speculations, and decline in the level of confidence especially amongst the men and women who worked in and around the World Trade Center. Economically and socially speaking, the years between the February 26, 1993 and the September 11, 2001 terrorist attacks at the World Trade Center could be likened to a series of aftershocks following major earth tremors or volcanic eruptions in a densely populated city or region. That period of approximately eight years and seven months between the two attacks, was marked by frequent intervals of disruptions at places of employment or work environment resulting from several false alarms of more suspected terrorist attacks. Each of those false alarms created more fears in the minds of the workers, psychologically weakens them both physically and mentally, and ultimately, exacerbates the condition of the economy.

Oftentimes in those uneventful days, some of the office buildings in the central business district (CBD) of New York City would be evacuated, and whenever that happens, it sends panics on the public within the surrounding environment. It was a period of a well-planned economic warfare by the terrorists on America's commercial capital, New York City, and it was a strategy used by the terrorists to distract and refocus the attention of the nation while they re-strategized for the bigger attacks that would occur just under nine years later.

The effects of the terrorists' economic warfare (directly and indirectly) led to a decline in average productivity as measured by output per man-hour and therefore, a decrease in the nation's gross domestic product (GDP); a measure of the economic health or economic well-being of a nation. In addition to this, there were many cases of psychological illnesses, particularly among the workforce or labor-force

Chapter Four

The September 11, 2001 Attacks

Otherwise known all around the world as the 9/11 (Nine-Eleven), the September 11, 2001 terrorists attacks that occurred simultaneously at three different locations on the east coast of the United States of America, took thousands of innocent lives in addition to destroying the nation's famous landmark, the World Trade Center (WTC). Particularly, the two elegant and magnificent architectural structures and exceptional landmarks within the WTC complex; Number One World Trade Center (1 WTC) and Number Two World Trade Center (2 WTC), which were popularly known to New Yorkers as the "Twin Towers", were completely destroyed beyond recognition as a result of the 9/11 atrocities. Both towers collapsed within minutes of each other.

On the day of the attacks, although the North Tower (Number 1 World Trade Center) was struck approximately 17 minutes before the South Tower (Number 2 World Trade Center), the later was the first to collapse at 9:59 a.m., but it took about 30 minutes later before the North Tower collapsed at 10:28 a.m. According to the timeline of the 9/11 events as produced by the Miller Center at the University of Virginia (The Miller at UVA), American Airlines Flight 11 took-off from Boston Logan International Airport at approximately 7:59 am with 76 passengers, 11 crew members, and 5 hijackers on board and was scheduled to land in Los Angeles, California on that day.

Subsequently (continued The Miller Report), United Airlines Flight 175 took off from the same Boston Logan International Airport at approximately 8:15 am on the same day with 59 passengers, 9 crew members and 5 hijackers on board, and was also heading for Los Angeles, California. At 8:20 a.m., American Airlines Flight 77 took-off from Dulles Airport outside of Washington D.C., and headed for Los Angeles, California with 53 passengers, 6 crew members and 5 hijackers onboard. Meanwhile, on the American Airlines Flight 11 which took-off from Boston Logan International Airport at 7:59 a.m., one of the five hijackers onboard the aircraft,

Figure 3: Number One World Trade Center (the North Tower) seen in Flames after being struck by the hijacked American Airlines Flight 11 at 8:46 a.m. (EST) on Tuesday, September 11, 2001. (Courtesy of bureau.plus)

Mohamed Atta, had unintentionally alerted air traffic controllers in Boston of the attack, though he meant to address the passengers. After hearing Mohamed Atta's unintentional broadcast on Flight 11, the Boston Air Traffic Control alerted the United States Air Force's Northeast Defense Sector, who then mobilized the Air National Guard to follow the aircraft.

Figure 4: A hijacked United Airlines Flight 175 (originally scheduled to land in Los Angeles, California) is seen approaching Number 2 World Trade Center (the South Tower) before crashing into it at 9:03 a.m. (EST) on Tuesday, September 11, 2001. (Courtesy of pinterest.com.)

Later that morning, United Airlines Flight 93 took-off from Newark International Airport (Newark Liberty International Airport) in Newark, New Jersey at 8:42 a.m. after some delay and was headed for Los Angeles, California with 33 passengers, 7 crew members, and 4 hijackers onboard. Unbelievably and unexpectedly, at 8:46 a.m. on Tuesday September 11, 2001, while the World Trade Center tenants (employees of several business organizations) were settling into their offices upon arriving for the day's work, the hijacked American Airlines Flight 11 crashes into the North Tower of the World Trade

Center. All aboard the aircraft (76 passengers, 11 crew members, and the 5 hijackers) were killed and so were many employees of the World Trade Center, with several of them trapped above the 91st Floor. Seventeen minutes later at 9:03 a.m., hijacked United Airlines Flight 175 originally scheduled to land in Los Angeles, California crashed into the South Tower of the World Trade Center with all the 65 people onboard killed instantly, as well as unknown number of people in that Tower. Furthermore, at 9:37 a.m., one of the hijacked airplanes, American Airline Flight 77 crashes into the United States Defense Headquarters (The Pentagon) and all those onboard (including 53 passengers, 6 crew members, and 5 hijackers were killed instantly.

Figure 5: A hijacked United Airlines Flight 175 (originally scheduled to land in Los Angeles, California) is seen here few minutes before it crashed into Number 2 World Trade Center (the South Tower) at 9:03 a.m. (EST) on Tuesday, September 11, 2001. (Courtesy of aneta.org)

Lastly, the last of the four airplanes hijacked on September 11, 2001, United Airlines Flight 93 which likely targeted either the White House or the US Capitol (although its ultimate target was unknown), plowed into an open (empty) field in Shanksville, Pennsylvania. As narrated by the Miller Center at UVA (millercenter.org/ remembering-september-11-terrorist-attacks), at 10:18 a.m. on the day of the attacks, the then President of the United States, President George W. Bush authorizes that any non-grounded planes within the United States air-space, to be shut down on sight. However, at that time, the president's team was operating under the impression that one of the hijacked planes, United Airlines Flight 93 was still in the air. Much later on that day, Building Number 7 of the World Trade Center collapsed, and at 8:30 p.m. same day, President George W. Bush addressed the nation in light of all the events of that day. Altogether, 2,977 people were killed in the deadliest terrorist attacks in American history on September 11, 2001 (millercenter.org).

One of the most painful memories of the September 11, 2001 bombing of the World Trade Center is the fact that the terrorists used America's own resources, both human and material to destroy the nation's properties and took the lives of many innocent Americans. To carry out their evil acts, these demonic agents or agents of darkness hijacked American aircrafts filled with several gallons of American aviation fuel, and the flight crew members onboard the hijacked air planes to destroy American lives and properties. Indeed, it felt like "a slap on the face". Moreover, the imbeciles were so bold to even aim at destroying the military headquarters of the most powerful nation in the world. The United States Military Headquarters, otherwise known as the Pentagon (so named after its unique architectural design, including its shape) is solidly built, very highly fortified and highly guarded. It's a location that any right-minded individual will not even attempt to go without a formal invitation by the military authorities.

As was the case with the World Trade Center first terrorist attack and bombing on February 26, 1993, the September 11, 2001 terrorist attack at the Pentagon left many people trapped in thick, blinding smoke as dark as soot. This caused several individuals who were trapped in the building to lose their sense of direction as they became disoriented due to the combined effects of smoke and soot, carbon monoxide, heat and fear, as well as other particulate matters that followed immediately after the attack. Simply put, there was pandemonium and what could be described as a state of higgledy-piggledy at that very moment. However, as the safety and law enforcement officers endeavored to rescue the trapped and disoriented individuals, those who heard their loud voices and headed toward them were led to safety and out of the building. Had it been that these individuals also lost their sense of hearing and direction and therefore become unable to hear the voices of the rescue team (the First Responders), or if they (the victims) had ignored the direction of the officers, then they would have also become a part of the statistics of the lost souls on that dreadful day.

However, one thing we must not forget is that the 9/11 terrorists/attackers were suicide bombers who had already decided to take their own lives and therefore believed that they would have nothing to lose by engaging in such daring/deadly acts. The only individual convicted in a United States court on criminal charges relating to the September 11, 2001 attacks, Zacarias Moussaoui, lost his bid to overturn his guilty plea. Moussaoui was sentenced to life imprisonment (without Parole) at a super-maximum-security prison in Colorado.

According to the CNN news agency, on July 31, 2024, the U.S. Government reached a plea deal with the alleged 9/11 terror attack mastermind, Khalid Sheikh Mohammed and two other defendants and co-conspirators (accused of plotting the September 11, 2001 terror attacks). The pretrial agreement (reached after twenty-seven months of negotiations) takes away the original death penalty imposed on Khalid Sheikh Mohammed, Walid Bin Attash, and Mustafa al Hawsawi. The news agency (Fox 5) added that shortly before the United States Department of Defense announced the news in a press release in the evening on Wednesday July 31, 2024, letters were sent to the families of the 9/11 victims and survivors. The plea agreement avoids what would have been a long and complicated death penalty trial against the 9/11 mastermind, Khalid Sheikh Mohammed. To the families and survivors of the 9/11 terror attack, this latest development (a plea deal) is an insult to injury and indeed, adds to their pain and emotional damage. All these happened because the United States

Government tried to determine how to handle the issue of torture used against Mohammed (the mastermind) and others at secret CIA prisons in the 2000s (the post 9/11 years).

In a later development based on Fox 5 News at 10 pm on Friday August 2, 2024, it was reported that the United States Defense Secretary, Lloyd Austin has rescinded the plea deal made with the 9/11 terror attack mastermind two days earlier and thereby, reinstating the death penalty as was originally imposed. The Defense Secretary added that the authority to make a decision on the plea deal rests solely on him. This latest move by Secretary Austin seems to be a move in the right direction and which could doubtless bring some level of relief to the families of the 9/11 victims and survivors. Unquestionably, any attempt to remove the death penalty on the 9/11 terror attack mastermind will indeed encourage more terror attacks on the United States soil.

It has been over two decades since the worst terrorist attacks on the United States soil occurred, but the death toll resulting from those attacks has continued to rise, including those who are losing their lives to the 2/26 and 9/11 related illnesses. According to the CBSN New York (Channel 10) News Network, on September 7, 2021, the death of the 1,647[th] person to die from the 9/11 terrorist bombing was recorded. Similarly, on June 2, 2022, the

ABC Channel 7 News (at 11 p.m. Eastern Standard Time, EST) in New York, announced that as of the date of that announcement that a total of 287 members of the New York Fire Department (firefighters) have died from the September 11, 2001 World Trade Center terrorist attack related illnesses. (As of September 2023, that number stood at 343, surpassing the number that died on the day of the attack.) These were a component of the service men and women who responded first to the incident and are otherwise known as the "First Responders". As of the time of going to the press, there are still several individuals who are sick from the 9/11 related illnesses and the death toll is likely to be rising as the years go by.

So far, the number of Fire Fighters who died from the 9/11-related illnesses has reached as much as the number that died on the day of the attack. In the first eight months of the Year 2023 alone, a total of 43 Fire Fighters died from the September 11, 2001-related illnesses. Also, 184 military personnel died at the United States Military Headquarters (the Pentagon) when the airplane hijacked by the terrorists struck the building on September 11, 2001.

Chapter Five

The Socioeconomic Implications of The 2/26 And 9/11 Terrorists Bombings And Attacks

The years immediately following the February 26, 1993 and the September 11, 2001 terrorist attacks, respectively, could be better described as "the eras of economic and psychological warfare" or better still, "the eras of aftershocks", and which, indeed, represented the aftershocks of those horrible events.

These uneventful events of February 26, 1993 and September 11, 2001 have made many Americans to become more aware of their surroundings and security conscious, and at the same time, reducing their level of trust for other persons. In the weeks and months following these attacks, New Yorkers, out of pre-cautious sense of security, became unusually anti-social and somehow unfriendly to strangers. Now more than ever, it is imperative that we become more conscious of who is standing next to us and be aware of our surroundings; we must be very vigilant. The pride of liberty is internal vigilance; New Yorkers be vigilant. Months following the September 11 2001 terrorist attacks, there were several incidences of suicide bombings as the United States endeavored to hunt down the terrorists, including the master-minders. However, a major concern these days with respect to security consciousness, particularly for the younger generation, is distraction from the social media and other electronic gadgets. This, indeed, has made so many young adults and teenagers unaware of their surroundings and thereby giving room to the enemy and become more vulnerable to terror attacks and other social ills.

In the case of the February 26, 1993, a.k.a. the 2/26 attack, the World Trade Center community and environ were completely changed particularly, concerning the peaceful gathering of people from various nationalities, cultures and ethnicities on the Trade Center Plaza during lunch hours. Immediately following that first terrorist attack at the Trade Center, many tenants (businesses) located in the Twin Towers relocated, some temporarily for several months (including the New York State Agency I worked for, the New York Metropolitan Transportation

Council, NYMTC), and others permanently to various suburban locations in the New York Metropolitan Area. Also, many employees of the organizations that were located in the Twin Towers (including myself), resigned from their employments for precautionary measures. My office was then located on the 82nd Floor East, in Number One World Trade Center, the North Tower (the same side the September 11 attack airplanes struck the building in approximately eight years and seven months later. While working at the World Trade Center before the 9/11 terrorist attack, I usually start my day's work in the office at 8:30 a.m. (Eastern Standard Time, EST), and the terrorists struck the building (with the hijacked airplane) at 8:46 a.m. on that uneventful day.

At several business locations in Manhattan (New York, New York) and particularly following the September 11 attacks, there were a series of wasteful, cost-generating fire drills that ordinarily should not have been conducted. There were several false alarm evacuations which kept management and staff always on their toes and always ready to exit the business premises instead of focusing on their duties. We had several of such unnecessary fire drills at my place of work at that time at the MTA Metro-North Railroad (near the Grand Central Terminal). I could recall some instances when some individuals, out of fear that another attack could happen, would not return to work after the fire drills and particularly, when such drills occur towards the end of the work day. It was indeed a form of psychological/economic warfare the enemies (terrorists) were using against the United States economy.

In reality, there was a significant decline in the average level of productivity per man-hour in the metropolitan New York area as fears of the unknown, and of the threats of another possible terrorist attacks over-took the minds of the people. (Literarily speaking, people became brain-washed with the threat of terrorism.) Undoubtably, the dual psychological and economic effects of the February 26, 1993 and the September 11, 2001 made a significant adverse impact on the economic health of the United States as measured with its gross domestic product (GDP). For the sake of those who are not in the field of economics, GDP is defined as the market value of all goods and services produced in a country in one year. At the same time, it gave the Peoples Republic of China the opportunity to advance its economy and get closer to the United States as the world's second largest economy and thereby, surpassing the nation of Japan which held that position for several years.

Psychology was nevertheless at work amongst the New York Metropolitan Area (New York Metro Area) workers and residents. Productivity per man-hour plunged drastically, while fear, frustration, discouragement, and discontentment became the order of the day amongst the urban workers. This decline in productivity subsequently caused instability in the price-level and ultimately inflation, hence there was a decrease in supply while demand continued to rise. In fact, one could literarily see clear evidences of the sense of hopelessness and disbelief on the faces of most New Yorkers in the months following the attacks. Particularly, at many of the major transportation terminals and more especially, the ones located in New York City's central business district (CBD) including the Grand Central Terminal (GCT), Times Square Station, Pennsylvania Station (Penn Station), the Port Authority Bus Terminal, and the Union Square Station, the atmosphere was often in a state of pandemonium as any unusual activities or movements in and around those areas made people to panic.

The sense of security was indeed very high at that time than I have ever observed in New York City for over four decades. Several residents of New York City and its environs relocated after the September 11, 2001 terrorist attack to the neighboring suburban areas. It was indeed horrific. In fact, this drift from the urban center to the suburban environments or de-urbanization (or sub-urbanization) created high (new) demand for commercial and residential real estate properties, as well as for other public/social services in the affected areas. Subsequently, there was excess supply of office/commercial units in the suburbs due to over-estimation of (panic) demand for commercial real estate. This eventually resulted in several units of those properties remaining vacant in the following years. At the same time, many commercial office spaces in the central business district (CBD) of New York City remained vacant.

Chapter Six

Summing It Up

The sad memories of the terrible and uneventful events of February 26, 1993 and September 11, 2001 in the United States will live with both Americans and peoples of the rest of the world for many generations to come. As of the publication of this book, increasing number of people who miraculously escaped the terminal effects of those attacks have been afflicted with one form of terminal disease or the other. Particularly, there has been increasing number of lung cancer cases amongst members of emergency rescue teams who were the first to respond to those tragic sites.

The very brave men and women who were the first to respond immediately following the attacks (the "First Responders") and their families are particularly going through serious emotional trauma till date, and many of these families have been devastated as a result of the after effects of the attacks and bombings. The inhalation of large volumes of toxic fumes, soot and other particulate matters has done and has continued to do, more physical, mental and psychological damages to the surviving victims of both the February 26, 1993 (2/26) and the September 11, 2001 (9/11) terrorist bombings and attacks at the World Trade Center in New York City.

To reiterate, the direct death tolls at and within the vicinities of the WTC stood at six lives (for the February 26, 1993) and 2,797 lives (for the September 11, 2001) terrorists attacks, respectively, and that number continues to grow even several years after the incidents. However, the focus has continued to be on 9/11 only. We must not be ignorant of the obvious fact that one life lost is one too many souls. It's absolutely imperative that the victims/survivors of 2/26 (of which I'm one of them) be recognized and honored and not be ignored nor forgotten by the Federal Government of the United States. So far, there have been a series of political debates at both the national and state levels on the 911 Victims Compensation Act otherwise known as the Never Forget the Heroes Act. Meanwhile, there has been little or no emphasis on any form of compensation fund for the victims and survivors of the 2/26/93 terrorist bombing and their families. Let's not forget nor disrespect these lost souls and their survivors, as well as those who in one way or another were harmed or injured from the bombing. No life is worth more than the other before God; we are all created equal.

The families affected by the February 26, 1993 terrorist bombing are no less valued than the families affected by the September 11, 2001 terrorist attacks.

The funds set aside by the Federal Government for the Compensation of the World Trade Center terrorists bombing victims and survivors continues to deplete as many new claims of the after-mats of the attacks continue to evolve. To date, issues surrounding the 9/11 victims' compensation (for individuals and families directly or indirectly injured due to the incident) continues to evolve. Many of the victims and their advocates argue that the fund allocated to the 9/11 Victims Compensation Fund by the US Federal Government is insufficient to adequately compensate all the victims (individuals who have developed or are developing 9/11 related illnesses). (Victims of the September 11, 2001 terrorist attacks may contact the 9-11 Victims Compensation Fund online at 911Victims.com or 911-Funds.com to apply for compensation Meanwhile, more 9/11 cancer related cases continue to emanate. According to the American Association for Justice, any individual who was present at the 9/11 crash site, Ground Zero or anywhere within the Lower Exposure Zone (in Lower Manhattan) between September 11, 2001 and May 30, 2002, and have been diagnosed with qualifying illness (including but, not limited to cancer) or injury, may be eligible for compensation through the Victim Compensation Fund (VCF).

On February 28, 2023, Senator Chuck Schumer, the US Senior Senator from New York, (on the NBC Channel 4 Evening News) requested that the US Federal Government should provide additional funds ($2 billion) needed to fully compensate all the victims of 9/11. So far, most of the 9/11 victims' compensation efforts have been focused on the First Responders who were directly affected by the attack, but not enough efforts have been made to thousands of individuals who were indirectly affected by the same act. For this cause, the Federal Government should endeavor to be fair and just in its efforts to ensure that the welfare of all the victims/survivors of these terrorist attacks in the United States are not taken for granted. They did not ask to die nor planned to die on those two horrific days and in the subsequent days following those terrorist bombings. They were innocent men and women who were patriotically serving their nation and humanity.

It is imperative, therefore, that the Federal Government, the respective states and local governments of the jurisdictions of the sites of the February 26, 1993 and the September 11 2001 terrorist attacks adequately respond to the needs and welfare of the first responders and survivors of these attacks as well as the welfare of their respective families.

The new (re-designed/re-built) One World Trade Center (also named the Freedom Tower, or 285 Fulton Street, New York, NY), although much taller than its predecessor, does not feature twin towers. With a height of 1,776 feet (probably to reflect the American Independence in the year 1776), the Freedom Tower represents the tallest building in the Western Hemisphere (including North America), and the second in the world after the Burj Khalifa in Dubai, United Arab Emirates (UAE), built in 2010 with a height of 2,717 feet. The Taipei 101 in Taipei City, Taiwan (with a height of 1,717 feet) now ranks the world's third tallest building, followed by the Willis Tower in Chicago, Illinois, USA. The actual construction of the Freedom Tower began in 2006. The new Number 2 World Trade Center, also known as 200 Greenwich Street, is yet to be built. When completed, it will occupy the position of the original Number 5 World Trade Center, and will represent the most energy-efficient office building in North America. The foundation work was completed in 2013 but the entire building has not been completed as of the time of going to the press.

Adequate networking, coordination and cooperation among all governmental agencies/authorities, including the police, firefighters, the FBI, the armed forces, etc., is imperative in order to avoid future surprises of terrorist attacks on the United States soil. One of the most talked about problems in dealing with the September 11, 2001 terrorist attacks at the World Trade Center and the United States Military Headquarters, the Pentagon, was the fight over supremacy and therefore, inadequate communication and cooperation among the various government authorities and law enforcement agencies particularly in the case of the attack on the World Trade Center.

It is also very important for the authorities to understand that these terrorists are not stupid but very clever (and street-smart) in their demonic acts and ideologies. They do not return immediately after any given attack; they wait until the law enforcement authorities have relaxed their efforts and indeed, the entire nation becomes distracted with other domestic/foreign issues for them to make a comeback. This is exactly what the terrorists did between the two attacks of February 26, 1993 and September 11, 2001; a period of approximately eight and a half years. We need to understand that the long-term period is a period for planning and adjustments in strategies and both the 2/26 and 9/11 terrorists used it to their selfish advantage. They (the terrorists) craftly and tactically used this period of "silence" to re-group, recuperate, and acquire or gather more relevant information for their next target(s) and also, to re-strategize their operations and re-state their Modus Operandi (MO). Let's not think that because the United States of America is the most powerful nation in the world and therefore become overconfident and relax over the issues of terrorism and foreign threats. It is also recommended that all the United States security/law enforcement agencies (the Secret Service, FBI, CIA, Homeland Security, states and other local law enforcement agencies) should endeavor to keep every plan designed to deal with any suspected act of terrorism absolutely secret and confidential until such plan is fully executed. When dealing with evil acts, including wars and terrorism, the idea of transparency, freedom of speech and freedom of information should be kept aside until the mission is completely accomplished. We must be careful and tactful so we do not equip the enemy.

All in all, we must all remain patriotic and vigilant in the fight against terrorism. Also, it is absolutely necessary for the entire world to understand the obvious reality that terrorism anywhere is terrorism everywhere. We are all in this together. Together and united we stand to conquer any enemy, but divided we become more vulnerable and eventually fall prey to the evil-minded ones. We must confront and combat the common enemy as a united force irrespective of our color, race or creed. According to the New York City Police Department's (NYPD) famous slogan, "If You See Something, Say Something"; be vigilant at all times.

We should endeavor to remain vigilant and be aware of our surroundings at all times in our present society. The world has changed and will continue to change, and we the people must therefore become very dynamic in dealing with the issues of our modern society. The idea of status quo should be scrapped if we must survive in this present age. A soldier does not sleep in the battlefield nor turn his/her back on the enemy and not until the battle is won. A famous African Head of State once cautioned his people while the nation was passing through a very challenging period in history and stated as follows: "The pride of liberty is internal vigilance; ___be vigilant".

The worst enemy is the enemy within. In reality, and as the Book of books, the Holy Bible, tells us, "There is no peace for the wicked". Anyone who hates peace, shall never experience peace; peace will elude such individual irrespective of their religious faith, nationality, ethnicity, color, creed, age or gender. He who lives by the sword, shall die by the sword. One life lost, is one too many. On Sunday February 26, 2023, at the commemoration of the 30th anniversary/remembrance of the February 26, 1993 terrorist bombing of the World Trade Center, the United States Senior Senator from New York, Senator Chuck Schumer, stated that "the September 11, 2001 terrorist attack has become a shorthand for a major reflection point in the American history". He then added that "that does not make the February 26, 1993 (bombing) less important".

There is, indeed, a need for equity and fairness for all. What is good for the geese is also good for the gander.

Finally, I will not fail to re-emphasize/reiterate the obvious fact that the United States has many enemies all over the world and the earlier every American (whether indigenous or foreign-born) understand and become more conscious of this fact, the more we will develop a better sense of vigilance. Let's be very clear, and know that the adversary (the enemy) wonders about like a roaring lion looking for who he may devour. Let's therefore not give any room to the adversary to take us by surprise anymore. We must be on guard at all times, in season and out of season so that we don't lose more innocent lives from similar incidents in the future. Bear in mind that we are referencing once living souls created by God in His own image and not to a carpenter's logs or lumbers. Enough is enough. One life lost is one too many.

References/Further Information

American Association for Justice, 9/11 Victims Compensation Fund. 911victims.com or 911-Funds.com.

Anderson, Dale (2004), Landmark Events in American History. The Terrorist Attacks of September 11, 2001, World Almanac Library, USA.

CBSN New York, Channel 10 Evening News (September 7, 2021). 9/11 Bombing.

CNN News Agency (August 2, 2024).

Fox 5 News at 10 (August 2, 2024).

Olshan, Jeremy, (Tuesday, January 5, 2010), Towering Over'em All. New York Post.

Tarshis, Lauren, (2011), I Survived Hurricane Katrina, 2005. Scholastic Inc. USA.

The Miller Center at University of Virginia, UVA, millercenter.org/remembering-september-11-terrorist-attacks.

Wikipedia, The Free Encyclopedia, en.wikipedia.org/wiki/2 World Trade Center.

__________,1993 World Trade Center Bombing. en.wikipedia.org/wiki/1993 World Trade Center bombing.